Sand and Shells

By Sascha Goddard

I run on the sand.

I will run up that hill, too!

hill

Sall will dig and fill this pot with sand.

The sun is hot.

Dell will get his hat.

hat

Bill will look for a crab.

Look at its legs and shell!

shell

legs

Look, a gull!

Gulls go up and yell a lot.

gull

Cass will look for shells till she gets ten.

Cass will set the shells on a big sand hut.

sand hut

Jill will swim till she huffs and puffs.

Jill swims well.

Huff, puff!

I had fun!

I will miss it here!

CHECKING FOR MEANING

1. What did Sall put in the bucket? *(Literal)*

2. Where did Cass put the shells she found? *(Literal)*

3. Do you think the girl in the text lives near the beach? Why? *(Inferential)*

EXTENDING VOCABULARY

fill	What does it mean to *fill* a container? What word do we use to describe a container that has been completely filled? I.e. full. What is the opposite of full?
yell	Look at the word *yell*. What is another word in the book that rhymes with *yell*?
till	What does *till* mean in this text? Explain to students that this can be used as a short form of the word *until*. Ask students if they know any other meaning of this word, e.g. as a place to store money.

MOVING BEYOND THE TEXT

1. What can you see and hear at the beach?

2. What animals might you find at the beach?

3. How does the water feel when you splash in the waves?

4. What can you do to stay safe at the beach?

SPEED SOUNDS

ff	ll	ss	zz

PRACTICE WORDS

will

hill

Sall

Bill

fill

Dell

gull

yell

shell

till

miss

well

Cass

Jill

huffs

puff

Gulls

puffs

shells

Huff